INSIDE ART MOVEMENTS

Romanticism

Susie Brooks

COMPASS POINT BOOKS
a capstone imprint

Compass Point Books are published by Capstone,
1710 Roe Crest Drive, North Mankato, Minnesota 56003
www.mycapstone.com

Library of Congress Cataloging-in-Publication Data
Names: Brooks, Susie, author.
Title: Romanticism / by Susie Brooks.
Description: North Mankato, Minnesota : Compass Point Books, a Capstone
imprint, [2020] | Series: Inside art movements | Audience: 9-14. |
Audience: 4 to 6.
Identifiers: LCCN 2018060765 | ISBN 9780756562403 (hardcover)
Subjects: LCSH: Romanticism in art--Juvenile literature. | Art, Modern—19th
century—Juvenile literature.
Classification: LCC N6465.R6 B76 2020 | DDC 709.03/42—dc23
LC record available at https://lccn.loc.gov/2018060765

Editorial credits
Series editor: Julia Bird
Designer: Mo Choy Design Ltd.
Image research: Diana Morris

Image artwork credits:
front cover. Caspar Friedrich, Wanderer Above a Sea of Fog, c.1818, oil on canvas,98.4 x
74.8 cm, Kunsthalle, Hamburg. Pictorial Press/Alamy. 1. Caspar Friedrich, Wanderer
Above a Sea of Fog, c.1818, oil on canvas, 98.4 x 74.8 cm, Kunsthalle, Hamburg.
Pictorial Press/Alamy. 4. Eugène Delacroix, Fantasia Arabe, 1833, oil on canvas, 60.5 x
74.5 cm, Städel Museum, Frankfurt. De Agostini/Superstock. 5t. Caspar Friedrich, The
Tree of Crows, c. 1822, oil on canvas, 59 x 73 cm, The Louvre, Paris. Artepics/age
fotostock/Superstock. 5b. JMW Turner, The Fighting Temeraire, 1838, oil on canvas, 91
x 122 cm, National Gallery, London. Bridgeman Art Library/Superstock. 6. Francois
Boucher, The Bird Catchers, 1784, oil on canvas, 294 x 337.8 cm, J. Paul Getty Museum,
Los Angeles. J Paul Getty Museum Open Content Program/PD/Wikimedia Commons.
7t. Jacques-Louis David, The Oath of the Horatii, 1784, oil on canvas, 329.8 x 424.8 cm,
The Louvre, Paris. Bridgeman Art Library/Superstock. 7b. Claude Joseph Vernet, The
Shipwreck, 1772, oil on canvas, 113.5 x 162.9 cm, National Gallery of Art, Washington,
D.C. Peter Barritt/Superstock. 8. Henri Fuseli, The Nightmare, 1781, oil on canvas, 101.6
x 126.7 cm, Detroit Institute of Arts. PD/Wikimedia Commons. 9t. William Blake,
Newton, 1795-c 1805, color print, ink and watercolor on paper, 40 x 60 cm, Tate,
London. Prisma-Album/Superstock. 9b. Goya, The Sleep of Reason Produces
Monsters, 1799, etching with aquatint and other intaglio media, 18.9 x 15 cm, Nelson
Atkins Museum, Kansas City. PD/Wikimedia Commons. 10. Jacques-Louis David,
Napoleon Crossing the Alps, 1800-1, oil on canvas, 261 x 221 cm, Château de
Malmaison, Rueil-Malmaison. 4 x 5 Collection/Superstock. 11t. Théodore Géricault,
The Charging Chasseur, 1812, oil on canvas, 349 x 266cm, The Louvre, Paris.
Masterpics/Alamy. 11b. Antoine-Jean Gros, Napoleon on the Battlefield of Eylau,
1808, oil on canvas, 104.9 x 145.1 cm, The Louvre, Paris.Fine Art Images/Alamy. 12.
Francisco Goya, The 3rd of May 1808, 1814, oil on canvas, 268 x 347 cm, El Prado,
Madrid. A. Burkatovski/Fine Art Images/ Superstock. 13. Francisco Goya, Qué alboroto
es este? (What is this tumult?)1814-15, etching, burnished aquatint, 17.5 x 22cm,
Metropolitan Museum of Art, New York. PD/MMNY. 14. Caspar Friedrich, The Cross in
the Mountains, 1808. Frame by Kühn after Friedrich's design, oil on canvas, 115 x 110.5
cm, Galerie Neue Meister, Dresden. De Agostini/Superstock. 15t. Jen Juels, Attempt
to Paint the Aurora Borealis, 1790s, oil on canvas, 31.2 x 39.5 cm, Ny Carlberg
Glyptotek, Copenhagen. Diderot/CC Wikimedia Commons. 15b. Phillip Otto Runge,
Morning, 1808, oil on canvas, 106 x 81 cm, Kunsthalle, Hamburg. Historic Images/
Alamy. 16. John Constable, Flatford Mill from a Lock on the Stour, c.1811, oil on canvas,
24.8 x 29.8 cm, Victoria and Albert Museum, London/Bridgeman Images. 17t. John
Constable, Study of Cirrus Clouds, c. 1822, oil on paper,11.4 x 17.8 cm, V & A Museum,
London. Victoria and Albert Museum, London/Bridgeman Images. 17b. John Crome,
The Poringland Oak, oil on canvas, 125.1 x 100.3 cm, Tate London. The History
Collection/Alamy. 18. Franz Pforr, Shulamit and Maria, 1810, oil on panel, 34 x 32cm,
Private Collection. PD/Wikimedia Commons. 19t. Perugino, Jesus Christ Giving the
Keys to St Peter, 1481-2, fresco, 335 x 550 cm, Sistine Chapel, Vatican. A. Burkatovski/
Fine Art Images/Superstock. 19b. Peter von Cornelius, Joseph Makes himself known to
his Brothers, 1817, fresco, 236 x 290 cm, Staatliche Museen, Berlin. A Burkatovski/Fine
Art Images/Superstock. 20. Théodore Géricault, The Raft of the Medusa, 1818-19, oil
on canvas, 491 x 716 cm, The Louvre, Paris. Bridgeman Images/Superstock. 21t. JMW

Turner, The Wreck of a Transport Ship, 1805-10, oil on canvas, 173 x 241 cm, Museu
Calouste Gulbenkian, Lisbon.   Iberfoto/Superstock. 21b. JMW Turner, The
Slave Ship, 1840, oil on canvas, 123 x 91 cm, Museum of Fine Arts, Boston. ACME
Imagery/Superstock. 22. Caspar Friedrich, Wanderer Above a Sea of Fog, c.1818, oil on
canvas, 98.4 x 74.8 cm, Kunsthalle, Hamburg. Pictorial Press/Alamy. 23t. Caspar
Friedrich, Two Men Contemplating the Moon, 1825-30, oil on canvas, 34.9 x 43.8 cm,
Metropolitan Museum of Art, New York. Acme Imagery/Superstock. 23b. Johan
Christian Dahl, Mother and Child by the Sea, 1840, oil on canvas, 21 x 31 cm, Barber
Institute of Arts, Birmingham. PD/Wikimedia Commons. 24. John Constable, The
Haywain, 1821, oil on canvas, 130.2 x 185.4 cm, National Gallery, London. Artepics/age
fotostock/Superstock. 25. JMW Turner, Norham Castle, c. 1822-3, watercolor on paper,
15.6 x 21.6cm, Tate, London. Oronoz/Album/Superstock. 26. Francisco Goya, Time and
the Old Women, 1810-12, oil on canvas, 181 x 125 cm, Musée des Beaux Arts, Lille.
Bridgeman Art Library/Superstock. 27t. Francisco Goya, Charles IV and his Family,
1800-01, oil on canvas, 280 x 336 cm, El Prado, Madrid. Bridgeman Art Library/
Superstock. 27b. Théodore Géricault, Woman Suffering from Obsessive Envy, 1822, oil
on canvas, 72 x 58 cm, Musée des Beaux Arts, Lyon. De Agostini/Superstock. 28.
James Ward, A Lion and Tiger Fighting, 1797, oil on canvas, 101.6 x 136.2 cm, The
Fitzwilliam Museum, Cambridge. Fitzwilliam Museum, Cambridge/Bridgeman Images.
29t. Horace Vernet, The Start of the Race of the Riderless Horses, 1820, oil on canvas,
46 x 54 cm, Metropolitan Museum of Art, New York. ACME Imagery/Superstock. 29b.
Edwin Landseer, Alpine Mastiffs Reanimating a Distressed Traveler, 1820, oil on canvas,
189 x 237 cm, Private Collection. 3LH/Superstock. 30. Eugène Delacroix, Massacre at
Chios, c.1824, oil on canvas, 422 x 353 cm, Musée du Louvre, Paris. Bridgeman Art
Library/Superstock. 31. Eugène Delacroix, Liberty Leading the People, 1830, oil on
canvas, 260 x 335 cm, Musée du Louvre, Paris. 4 x 5 Collection/Superstock. 32.
Anne-Louis Girodet de Roucy (Girodet-Trioson), The Revolt at Cairo, 1810, oil on
canvas, 365 x 500 cm, Chateaux de Versailles et de Trianon. PD/Wikimedia Commons.
33t. Eugène Delacroix, Women of Algiers in their Apartment, 1834, oil on canvas, 180
x 229 cm, Musée du Louvre, Paris. Fine Art Images/Superstock. 33b. Théodore
Chasseriau, Battle of Arab Horsemen Around a Standard, 1852, oil on canvas, 53.9 x
63.9 cm, Dallas Museum of Art, Texas. Foundation for the Arts Collection, Mrs John
B.O'Hara Fund/Bridgeman Images. 34. John Martin, The Great Day of His Wrath,
1851-3, oil on canvas, 196.5 x 303.2 cm, Tate, London. Artepics/age fotostock/
Superstock. 35t. Karl Briullov, The Last Day of Pompeii, 1833, oil on canvas, 465.5 x 651
cm, The Russian Museum, St Petersburg. PD/Wikimedia Commons. 35b. JMW Turner,
Shade and Darkness, The Evening of the Deluge, 1843, oil on canvas, 78.5 x 78,1 cm,
Tate London. Art Collection 2/Alamy. 36. François Rude, Departure of the Volunteers
of 1792 (La Marseillaise), 1833-6, limestone, 12.8m x 7.9 m, L'Arc de Triomphe, Paris.
Bridgeman Art Library/Superstock. 37t. Auguste Préault, Killing, modelled 1834, cast
1850, bronze, 109 x 140 cm, Musée des Beaux Arts, Chartres. Le Passant/CC
Wikimedia Commons. 37b. Antoine-Louis Barye, Tiger Surprising an Antelope, c.1835,
bronze, 38.7 x 58 x 30.7 cm, Dallas Museum of Art, Texas. Adrien Lenoir/CC
Wikimedia Commons. 38. Johann Zoffany, The Academicians of the Royal Academy,
1771-2, oil on canvas, 101 x 147 cm, The Royal Collection Trust. De Agostini/
Superstock. 39t. Constance Marie Charpentier, Melancholy, 1801, oil on canvas, 130 x
165 cm, Musée de Picardie, Amiens. PD/Wikimedia Commons. 39b. Marie Ellenrieder,
Christ in the Temple, 1849, oil on canvas, 166 x 105.8 cm, Osborne House, IOW. Royal
Collection Trust/© Her Majesty Queen Elizabeth II 2018. 40. Frederick Church,
Niagara, 1857, oil on canvas, 101.6 x 229.8 cm, National Gallery of Art, Washington D.C.
Corcoran Collection/NGA Washington D.C./Bridgeman Images. 41t. Thomas Cole,
Desolation (The Course of Empire), 1836, oil on canvas, 100.3 x 161.2 cm, New York
Historical Society. PD/Wikimedia Commons. 41b. Hans Gude, View Across Fjord, 1859,
oil on canvas, 130 x 170 cm, Kunstmuseum, Bergen. The History Collection/Alamy. 42.
Gustave Courbet, The Stone Breakers, 1849, oil on canvas, 159 x 259 cm, Galerie Neue
Meister Dresden, destroyed 1945. © Staatliche Kunstsammlungen Dresden/
Bridgeman Images. 43t. Jean Baptiste Camille Corot, The Gust of Wind, 1865-70, oil
on canvas, 48 x 66 cm, Pushkin Museum, Moscow/Bridgeman Images. 43b. John
Everett Millais, Ophelia, 1851-2, oil on canvas, 76.2 x 111.8 cm, Tate London.
Superstock. 44t. Odilon Redon, Chariot of Apollo, c. 1908, oil on canvas, 100 x 80 cm,
Musée des Beaux Arts, Bordeaux. PD/Wikimedia Commons. 44b. Graham
Sutherland, Western Hills, 1938-41, oil on canvas, 55.5 x 90.5 cm, National Galleries of
Scotland, Edinburgh. © The Estate of Graham Sutherland 2018. Bridgeman Images. 45.
Claude Monet, Stormy Sea at Étretat, 1883, oil on canvas, 100 x 81 cm, Musée des
Beaux Arts, Lyon. PD/Wikimedia Commons.

First published in Great Britain in 2018 by Wayland
Copyright © Hodder & Stoughton, 2018

All internet sites appearing in back matter were available and accurate when
this book was sent to press.

Printed and bound in China.
1593

Table of Contents

The Art of Awe

When you see the word *Romanticism*, you might think of hearts and flowers. But in art, Romanticism had nothing to do with this—it was all about drama, sensation, glory, imagination, and the awesome (and awful) wonders of life!

What is Romanticism?

Romanticism began as a movement in literature but quickly spread to art and music. In the late 1700s, writers in Europe started to challenge the very rational way of thinking that was popular at the time. They wanted to write about uncontrolled emotions, such as hope, despair, fear, and anger. Artists soon saw the thrill in this too, filling their paintings with a new sense of passion.

Fantasia Arabe, Eugène Delacroix, 1833

Rights and Revolution

The Romantics were stirred by unsettled times in Europe. During a period called the Enlightenment (c. 1650–1800), people became motivated by knowledge and reason and the fact that they could think as individuals. They wanted equal rights for everyone, not special privileges for rulers or the church. One of the biggest outcomes of this era was the French Revolution (1789–1799), an uprising of ordinary people that toppled France's monarchy and led to a series of wars.

Heart Over Mind

The spirit of revolution excited the Romantics, but they resented the Enlightenment's focus on reason and order. This appeared in art in a movement called neoclassicism, which revived ideas from ancient Greece and Rome. The Romantics felt that this grand but rigid style was too flawless to express real experiences. They wanted to paint with their hearts, not their minds— and they went about this in very individual ways.

The Tree of Crows, Caspar David Friedrich, 1822

Who, What, Where?

The power of nature was a favorite subject for the German artist Caspar Friedrich (above) and British artists John Constable and J.M.W. Turner (below). They lifted landscape art to a new level of importance, often sketching outdoors. Francisco Goya in Spain and Eugène Delacroix in France (far left) loved to paint real-life drama, while dreams and events from the Bible were popular Romantic themes too. Beyond the main centers of Germany, France, and Britain, Romanticism spread to other parts of Europe and the U.S.

The Fighting Temeraire, J.M.W. (Joseph Mallord William) Turner, 1839

"Romanticism is precisely situated neither in choice of subject nor in exact truth, but in a way of feeling."
Charles Baudelaire, 19th century writer

Look Closer

Romantic art is difficult to define because there was no single subject or style. Look at the three very different images on this page. Can you see what they have in common? Think about what the artists were trying to communicate.

The Pendulum Swings

Like a pendulum, artistic tastes moved back and forth in the 1700s and early 1800s. Romanticism sprung up to challenge stern neoclassicism, which in itself was a reaction to more exuberant styles that had come before!

The Bird Catchers, François Boucher, 1748

Frivolous Rococo

In the mid-1700s in Europe, rococo was the dominant style. Artists like Boucher (above) painted flamboyant, playful scenes, full of color and fashionable people doing fashionable things. The neoclassicists found this far too extravagant—they wanted discipline and intellect! Like other Enlightenment thinkers, they looked back to classical Greece and Rome for more rational and harmonious ideas.

Formal Neoclassicism

The neoclassicists believed in strong drawing, accurate shading, and a perfectly smooth paint finish. Obeying traditional rules of perspective, they created a realistic sense of space on their canvases. They chose somber colors and historic subjects arranged in balanced compositions. The result was a sense of calm monumentality, as you can see in the painting of Romans by Jacques-Louis David (top right).

Oath of the Horatii, Jacques-Louis David, 1784

Rebellious Romantics

Neoclassicism began around 1760, and it wasn't long before the pendulum swung again. Over the next few decades, some artists started making more chaotic or dramatic work, like Vernet's shipwreck below. They sowed the seeds of Romantic art, which stood for impulse and emotion, not order and calm. Richer colors, expressive brushstrokes, and theatrical compositions were all traits of this new boisterous style.

The Shipwreck, Claude-Joseph Vernet, 1772

Look Closer

Romanticism matched Neoclassicism in techniques like perspective and proportion. But can you see a difference in mood between these paintings by David and Vernet? Which has more energy? What creates this feeling? Look at the colors, brushwork, and dominant lines in the works.

Parallel Movements

Romanticism never eclipsed neoclassicism but instead developed alongside it. In those days artistic taste was governed by official art academies, especially those in Paris and London. Their members argued over which style was best to follow, often favoring neoclassicism for its polished, idealized look. They also held huge annual exhibitions, which were the best chance for any artist to become known.

Dreams and Visions

Think about your imagination—you don't have much control over it! The Romantics believed that creativity came from a subconscious, unthinking place. Some early Romantic artists showed this by painting dreamlike or visionary scenes.

The Nightmare, Henry Fuseli, 1781

Fuseli's Nightmare

Henry Fuseli was a Swiss painter who spent much of his life in Britain. He was fascinated by dreams, the supernatural, and things that we can't logically explain. Fuseli wanted his paintings to shock and intrigue people, and he succeeded when he created *The Nightmare* (above). This ghoulish scene came from Fuseli's imagination, as well as ideas from folklore and classical art.

Look Closer

To interpret this painting, we need to use our imagination. How do you feel when you look at it? What role do you think the demon plays? What about the horse in the background?

Gothic Horror

Fuseli drew inspiration from literature, including witch and fairy themes from William Shakespeare (1564–1616). His paintings in turn inspired writers like Mary Shelley (1797–1851), who wrote the novel *Frankenstein*. This book was part of a trend called gothic horror, which began in the late 1700s with stories of ghosts and the grotesque. People were growing hungry for tales of weirdness and wonder, in contrast to Enlightenment reason.

Blind Science

William Blake was a British writer and artist who, like many Romantics, considered himself a visionary (able to see things that others couldn't). He believed that rational thinking was bad because it dulled people's instincts and stopped them looking for change. His painting of Isaac Newton (right) highlights this by suggesting that the scientist can't see beyond his paper and compass. He sits in darkness and is blind to creativity, represented by the colorful rock behind him.

Isaac Newton, William Blake, 1795–c.1805

"Art is the Tree of Life. Science is the Tree of Death."

William Blake

The Sleep of Reason Produces Monsters, Francisco Goya, 1797–1799

The Sleep of Reason

This etching by Francisco Goya also explores Enlightenment thinking in an interesting way. First, when reason sleeps—monsters appear! This could be seen as a positive thing, unleashing the artist's creativity. But Goya was also impatient with people's superstitions and felt that reason was needed to override them. He seems to be warning us not to be ruled by rationality or imagination alone.

Battling for Glory

Dreams and nightmares were one thing, but the Romantics faced turmoil in reality too. They worked in the wake of the French Revolution, as Napoleon Bonaparte rose to power in France and began waging war across Europe.

The Rise of Napoleon

Napoleon was an army general who charged to success in support of the French Revolution. The revolutionaries wanted freedom and equality for ordinary people, and they managed to snatch power from both the king and the Roman Catholic Church. But they ended up with another supreme ruler—in 1799, Napoleon overthrew the government and in 1804 declared himself Emperor of France.

Napoleon Crossing the Alps, Jacques-Louis David, 1800–1801

Painted Glory

Napoleon was obsessed with power and image, and he employed artists to glorify him on canvas. They portrayed him as a hero as he invaded other countries and gradually gained control of most of the continent. He was the ultimate symbol of Romanticism—dangerous, determined, and battling the forces of nature as well as human armies. This painting (above) by David celebrates his grueling journey across the Alps to conquer Italy.

Contrasting Styles

David's painting is Romantic in feeling but mostly neoclassical in style. Although the horse is rearing and Napoleon's cape is flying, the effect is still controlled and static. Compare this to Théodore Géricault's frenzied image of one of Napoleon's cavalry officers (right). He swivels around as his horse dives away, sweeping in a diagonal across the canvas. The brushstrokes look vigorous and dramatic too, typical of Romanticism.

The Charging Chasseur, Théodore Géricault, 1812

Napoleon on the Battlefield of Eylau, Antoine-Jean Gros, 1808

Facing Reality

This painting (left) by Antoine-Jean Gros was a piece of propaganda for Napoleon. It shows him compassionately visiting the battlefield after a bloody French defeat over Russia. While Gros followed official instructions for the painting, he didn't try to hide the harsh reality. It is such a huge picture that the bodies in the foreground are twice life-size. We can see fear in the wounded soldiers' faces and feel the bite of the snow.

Look Closer

Gros was a pupil of Jacques-Louis David, but he broke away from idealized neoclassicism. What makes his painting more Romantic in mood?

A Storyteller in Spain

In 1808 Napoleon turned on Spain, ousted the king, and put his own brother on the throne. One artist who recorded the troubled times that followed was Francisco Goya.

A Bleak View

Goya was a court painter to the Spanish royal family, highly successful for his portraits. But he had a traumatic personal life, suffering the death of many of his children and an illness that made him deaf. His work became progressively more dark and gloomy, with a bleak or critical view of the world. This only increased when his country was plunged into war.

The Third of May 1808, Francisco Goya, 1814

Terror in May

On May 2, 1808, the people of Madrid rebelled against French troops occupying their city. The French crushed the uprising, rounded up the rioters, and shot them the following day. Goya captured these events in two of his most famous and compelling paintings. In the one above, the patriotic Spanish people face the firing squad.

Look Closer

Notice how Goya arranged the painting at left, with a strong line of gunmen in contrast to the crumbling crowd of victims. What else gives the picture its powerful, tragic effect?

Emotional Narrative

One of Goya's great talents as an artist was storytelling. He was excellent at painting emotion and individuality in people's expressions and poses. He also used color and light very dramatically, highlighting crucial points of the action. The intensity and anguish of his May 1808 paintings were groundbreaking in the history of art.

65

Qué alboroto es este?

What is this Hubbub? from *Disasters of War*, Francisco Goya, c.1814–1815 (published 1863)

Making a Mockery

Goya chronicled the events and beliefs of his time and often made fun of them too. He created many paintings and etchings that mocked local superstitions or other aspects of society. He also made a set of prints, including the one above, in reaction to the horrors of the Peninsular War (1808–1814). This was a fight for Spain and Portugal that followed Napoleon's invasion.

The Spirit of Nature

While war and rebellion were ravaging Spain, a different type of revolution happened in Germany. In 1808 Caspar David Friedrich opened his art studio to reveal his latest work. It was a religious altarpiece, dominated by a landscape—something extraordinary for the time.

Holy Scenery

Friedrich called his painting (at right) *The Cross in the Mountains*, though the crucifix is just a tiny part of the scene. It blends quietly into the pine-covered mountaintop under a cloudy but sun-streaked sky. Friedrich designed the frame himself, shaping it to hang at a chapel altar. Altarpieces traditionally showed close-up figures from the Bible—but here the figure of Christ on the cross is barely visible at all!

The Cross in the Mountains, Caspar David Friedrich, 1808

A Romantic Milestone

This was Friedrich's first large painting, and it shocked many people at first. Surely it was blasphemy to promote a landscape to the level of religion! But the altarpiece marked a milestone in Romanticism—the start of the rise of landscape art. Typically the academies gave landscapes a low rank, below history painting (including religious), genre painting (scenes of everyday life), and portraiture.

Landscape Art

It was actually a decline in religious art that helped landscape painting to grow. This began after the Protestant Reformation (1517–1648), when much of Europe broke from the Roman Catholic Church. In the 1600s, landscapes became popular in Dutch art, and elsewhere as idealized settings to history paintings. But only in the late 1700s and early 1800s did landscape painting really take off, as artists like Friedrich associated nature with God's creation, and growing industry threatened the countryside.

Landscape with Northern Lights, Jens Juel, 1790s

Morning I, Otto Runge, 1808–1809

A Spiritual Cycle

Friedrich studied at the Academy of Fine Arts in Copenhagen, where he learned from Danish painters such as Jens Juel (above). Another German student there was Otto Runge, who shared Friedrich's interest in the spiritual side of nature. His *Morning I* (left) was part of a cycle of paintings that he planned to show in a chapel, accompanied by choir music and poetry. Unfortunately this never materialized as he died young, before the project was finished.

"Everything is becoming more airy and light than before . . . everything gravitates towards landscape."

Otto Runge

Look Closer

Runge's picture is symbolic—it shows the light of morning as the spark of life from God in all of nature. Notice the new baby, lying on a bed of flowers in the foreground. Where do your eyes naturally lead when you look at this painting? Why do you think this is?

Embracing the Outdoors

What is the best way to experience the magnificence of nature? How do you paint the changing light and weather or the drama of a mountain view? The Romantic artists realized that to fully embrace the landscape, they needed to be outdoors.

Bulky Materials

Painting outdoors was a difficult business 200 years ago. Artists had to transport powdered pigments in glass vials or pigs' bladders and mix their own paints, which would dry out afterwards. They carried heavy wooden paint boxes and bulky paper or canvas, and had to work much more quickly than they were used to. Final paintings were done back indoors at the artist's studio.

Making Sketches

When artists are planning a painting, they usually make sketches first to help them decide what colors and viewpoints work best. In the 1600s and 1700s, painters were already going outside to do this. Usually they worked in pencil, ink, or watercolor for quick results— but the French landscapist Claude Lorrain (1600–1682) was one artist who is said to have sketched in oil paints too.

Study for *Flatford Mill from a Lock on the Stour*, John Constable, 1811

Oil Sketch Pioneer

The real pioneer of outdoor oil sketching was the English Romantic John Constable. While most artists sketched to record landscape features, Constable focused on the light and weather. He used bold colors and rapid brushwork and kept the spontaneous feel of his sketches when he completed a final painting (see above). This gave his work a fresh-from-nature feeling and led to sketches being seen as art in their own right.

The Science of Skying

Constable went on to practice what he called skying, painting clouds repeatedly at different times of day or year (below). He made detailed notes on the back of his sketches, logging things like the position of the sun and direction of the wind. The science of meteorology (weather) was very new back then, and Constable found it intriguing. His studies have since been used by geographers tracking air pollution and climate change.

Study of Cirrus Clouds, John Constable, 1822

The Poringland Oak, John Crome, 1818–1820

Observing Nature

Direct observation of nature was important to other Romantics too. Friedrich sketched outdoors in Germany, while John Crome of the Norwich School in England was one of the first artists to paint identifiable species of trees (right). J.M.W. Turner filled sketchbooks with atmospheric watercolor landscapes. And from 1841, the invention of resealable paint tubes made open-air work much easier for artists.

"The world is wide; no two days are alike, nor even two hours; neither were there ever two leaves of a tree alike since the creation of the world."

John Constable

A Brotherhood in Rome

In 1810 a group of artists from Germany moved to live in a disused monastery in Italy. They wanted to revive religious art from the Middle Ages—and they threw themselves into it, growing long hair and dressing in biblical clothes!

Christian Values

The artists first met at the Vienna Academy in Austria. In 1809 they formed the Brotherhood of Saint Luke, vowing to bring back the Christian values that they felt had been lost from recent painting. The following year, in the midst of Napoleon's upheaval in Europe, they traveled to the capital of Christian art—Rome. They were nicknamed the Nazarenes (a title sometimes used for Jesus) for the religious way that they lived.

Looking Back

Friedrich Overbeck and Franz Pforr were two founder members of the Nazarenes. Others joined them in Rome, including Wilhelm Schadow and Peter Cornelius. They rejected neoclassicism and the rules of the art academies, which they felt put artistic methods before good morals. Instead they looked back to Albrecht Dürer (1471–1528) and the golden age of German painting, as well as Italian Renaissance artists, such as Pietro Perugino (1446–1523) and Raphael (1483–1520).

Shulamit and Maria, Franz Pforr, 1810

Look Closer

The Nazarenes were Romantics because they wanted to show honesty and deeper meaning in their art. Often they did this with symbols. What references can you see to religion and friendship in this painting by Pforr at left?

Medieval Revival

The Nazarenes revived the medieval workshop system, as well as the art of fresco—painting directly onto wet plaster on a wall. You can see from Cornelius's fresco (bottom) and Pforr's panel painting how they imitated art like Perugino's (below). Their style was detailed and two-dimensional rather than focusing on realistic shading. The spiritual themes they chose, like many Romantics, were perhaps an antidote to war.

Jesus Christ Giving the Keys to St. Peter, Pietro Perugino, 1481–1482

Influential Art

Although they are little known today, the Nazarenes were very popular at the time. Their art soon caught on in Germany, where it became a national style. They influenced an Italian movement called purismo, as well as French artists, including the neoclassicist Jean-Auguste-Dominique Ingres, who spent time in Rome. In England especially, they had an important impact on another brotherhood—the Pre-Raphaelites.

The Recognition of Joseph by his Brothers, Peter Cornelius, 1816–1817

Shipwrecks and Storms

Imagine a raft crammed with terrified people, cast adrift on a ferocious sea. They fight, kill, and even eat the dead to survive. This happened to French sailors in 1816, and one Romantic painter later captured the action.

Scandalous Story

The *Medusa*, a French naval ship, had run aground off the coast of Africa without enough lifeboats. So the crew cobbled together a makeshift raft and some 150 people drifted off on it without supplies. When they were rescued 13 days later, only 15 were still alive and of these, five soon died. The tragedy made international news, two survivors wrote bestsellers—and Théodore Géricault saw a chance to make his name with an enormous painting.

The Raft of the Medusa, Théodore Géricault, 1818–1819

Lifelike Painting

Géricault interviewed survivors, visited morgues, and filled his studio with body parts to use as models. He made endless sketches and studies before arriving at the dynamic pyramid of figures in his scene (above). His final canvas, more than 22 feet long, is larger than life and starkly lit. It is so vividly painted that you might feel seasick just looking at it.

Across the Channel

In 1819 Géricault showed his raft painting at the Paris Salon, the official exhibition of the French Academy. Many people criticized his work, probably sensitive about the story—but it had a better reception the following year when Géricault took it to London. By this stage, Napoleon's reign of war had ended with the Battle of Waterloo (1815), and people could travel safely again. French and British artists started exchanging ideas.

The Wreck of a Transport Ship, J.M.W. Turner, 1805–1810

The Slave Ship, J.M.W. Turner, 1840

The Sublime Sea

One British painter who had a lifelong obsession with the sea was J.M.W. Turner. Like most Romantics, he saw nature as sublime—dangerous, terrifying, and awesome at the same time. He painted many storms and shipwrecks, both real and imaginary, including the two very different images on this page. The message was this—nature can turn without warning, and as humans we are no match for its power.

⋯⋯➤ *Look Closer*

Notice how Turner's style developed, becoming more abstract over the years. Which image do you think best conveys the drama and danger of a storm?

Moonlight and Mist

Of course nature wasn't always the wild, cruel force that destroyed human lives at sea. Some Romantic artists focused on the quiet side of the sublime—people contemplating peaceful but still awe-inspiring landscapes.

Lost in the Landscape

This wanderer (at right) painted by Friedrich has come a long way—about as far from urban life as he can! He is up on a peak like the king of a castle, but he looks strangely out of place in his smart coat and shoes. Although he is the central focus of the picture, he is dwarfed by the giant landscape looming in front of him. Alone and with his back turned to us, he seems lost in a mysterious private world.

A Unique View

We will never know exactly what Friedrich's wanderer is seeing—we share his view, but only from behind. Friedrich did this to suggest a unique experience and one man's outlook. Individual visions were crucial to Romantic artists, whether painting a mountaintop, shipwreck, or battle. They wanted to express their own viewpoint and put something of themselves in every work.

Wanderer Above the Sea of Fog, Caspar David Friedrich, 1818

Look Closer

How does Friedrich emphasise the forces of nature? What role do you think the fog or mist plays? How would it feel to be up on this mountain?

Deeper Meaning

Friedrich used back views in many other paintings, including several of people admiring the moon (right). He saw the moon and sky, watching over nature, as spiritual reminders of the presence of God. Sometimes he added coded political messages, such as the old-fashioned *altdeutsch* costume on his wanderer. This clothing was banned in Germany at the time because it had been worn by rebels who opposed the government.

Two Men Contemplating the Moon, Caspar David Friedrich, 1825–1830

Mother and Child by the Sea, Johan Christian Dahl, 1840

Norwegian View

The Norwegian artist Johan Christian Dahl moved to Germany and shared a house with Friedrich. You can see his friend's influence in this moonlit scene (at left), painted the year Friedrich died. A mother and child gaze out at a fishing boat— is it just arriving or leaving? The scene has a sense of wonder and hope as the moon casts reflections on the water.

"The artist should not only paint what he sees before him, but also what he sees within him. If, however, he sees nothing within him, then he should also omit to paint that which he sees before him."

Casper David Friedrich

Two Englishmen

The two greatest names in British Romantic art were hardly the greatest of friends! John Constable and J.M.W. Turner differed in almost every way, but they each made a vital mark on landscape painting.

The Hay Wain

In 1821 Constable painted *The Hay Wain* (below)—a big canvas showing a quiet rural landscape. He created it with the help of outdoor sketches and by using thick dabs and dashes of paint. This rough finish didn't appeal to conservative English viewers—but when Constable sent the painting to the Paris Salon in 1824, it won an important prize. The rich colors and lively brushstokes particularly impressed the French artist Delacroix.

The Hay Wain, John Constable, 1821

> *"Painting is but another word for feeling."*
> John Constable

Nostalgic View

Constable's idyllic scene has a feeling of nostalgia for the countryside. At the time it was painted, the British landscape was changing due to the Industrial Revolution (1760–c.1840). Expanding cities and new farming machinery were invading rural life. Constable was the son of a landowner and felt strongly about his local Suffolk scenery. He spent day after day immersed in this "Constable country," and never left England in his life.

Theatrical Turner

Turner, on the other hand, rose from humble beginnings and soon started traveling around Europe. He was a great self-promoter who even set up his own gallery to display his work at its best. Turner's art was more dramatic than Constable's, with a different type of energy and atmosphere. While Constable painted in a naturalistic way, Turner drenched his scenes in theatrical light.

Competitive Rivals

Constable and Turner were critical of each other's work and highly competitive too. At one Royal Academy exhibition in London in 1832, their works were hung side by side. Turner saw the vibrant colors, including red, in Constable's river scene, and he didn't want to be outdone. So at the last minute he added a dab of red to his pale seascape and managed to upstage his rival!

Norham Castle, on the River Tweed, J.M.W. Turner, c.1822

⋯⋯▶ Look Closer

Some people say that Constable's landscapes feel like a memory, while Turner's place us right there in the moment. Do you agree with this? What other differences do you notice between this watercolor by Turner and Constable's oil painting opposite?

"Indistinctness is my forte."
J.M.W. Turner

25

Baring the **Soul**

If we want to show what somebody looks like, it's easy to take a photograph. But the Romantics didn't have cameras! Photography was invented in the 1830s but only became popular around 50 years later. Before that, people relied on artists' portraits.

Old and Vain

Goya painted many grand portrait commissions for Spanish royals and other nobles. He also created far less complimentary images, like *Old Women (Time)* below. The lady in white is Queen Maria Luisa of Spain—we can tell because she wears the same jewelry in an earlier royal family portrait by Goya (above right). But here she is part of a warning against vanity, showing that looks don't last forever. The figure of Time is looming behind the women, having sneakily stolen their youth.

Portrait Patrons

Traditionally, portraits and other artworks were commissioned by buyers, known as patrons. This still happened during the Romantic age (in fact, it pushed the development of photography, as industrialization created more middle class people who wanted pictures). But as the Academy exhibitions gained importance, artists also made unsolicited work for anyone to buy. This helped them to paint more freely and expressively, without needing to flatter a particular person

Old Women/Time, Francisco Goya, c.1808–1812

Charles IV and His Family, Francisco Goya, 1800

Anonymous Faces

In 1822 Géricault painted a series of portraits like the one below for a doctor of mental health. No one is sure if they were commissioned or a gift, but either way they were not done to please the sitters. Géricault painted ten anonymous patients, each suffering from a different psychological condition. The doctor claimed he could spot their disorders just by looking at the pictures!

A Woman Suffering from Obsessive Envy (Portraits of the Insane), Théodore Géricault, 1822

Inner Suffering

Géricault painted these haunting portraits quickly and from life. His fast brushwork adds to the uneasy feeling, as do the strong contrasts between dark and light. All of the patients look away from the viewer as if lost in their own worlds. We can feel their inner suffering through the emotion on their faces—true to Romanticism, they are baring their soul.

Animal Magnetism

Just as human nature intrigued the Romantics, so did the character of animals. There was a growing interest in zoology at the time, as well as a tendency to see deep connections between people and all living things.

Down at the Zoo

It wasn't unusual to hear the roar of wild animals in European cities by the 1800s. What began as private menageries for the aristocracy became early zoos, where people could see lions, tigers, and other beasts shipped over from far-flung lands. Many artists, including Delacroix and Landseer, sketched at these places, and Romantic poets such as William Wordsworth and Lord Byron visited too. (Byron also kept a mix of animals, from dogs and horses to monkeys and peacocks, at his various homes.)

Fight between a Lion and a Tiger, James Ward, 1797

Look Closer

It's unlikely that James Ward ever saw a lion and tiger fighting, but he imagined how it would look. How has he created a sense of tense drama in the painting above? Look at the animals' positions, expressions, and the use of light, shade, and brushwork.

Superhuman Horses

Horses were a particular inspiration to the Romantics—in the days before motor vehicles, soldiers rode them into battle, and they were powerful working beasts. Géricault was a fanatical horseman (who died young, partly as a result of many riding accidents), and he made many heartfelt paintings of these animals. Delacroix also captured horses rearing, galloping, and interacting expressively with their owners.

The Start of the Race of the Riderless Horses, Horace Vernet, 1820

Untamed Energy

The above painting by Horace Vernet shows the start of a riderless horse race—the highlight of the yearly Carnival in Rome. We can see the animals' incredible strength as they struggle against their handlers. They are full of untamed energy—the inner fire that the Romantics loved to capture. Vernet was also one of several Romantic artists who illustrated Byron's "Mazeppa," a poem about a man being tied to a wild horse.

Alpine Mastiffs Reanimating a Distressed Traveler, Edwin Henry Landseer, 1820

Four-Legged Heroes

Edwin Henry Landseer is probably best known for his lion sculptures in London's Trafalgar Square. He was also unrivaled as an animal painter, able to capture the life and character of his subjects. This painting at left, which he made aged just 18, shows the dogs as heroic rescuers. It is full of suspense and movement as the animals bark and try to revive the fallen traveler.

A Passionate Painter

One of the most celebrated Romantic artists came into his own from the mid-1820s. Eugène Delacroix followed in the footsteps of his fellow Frenchman Géricault, who died in 1824.

Massacre at Chios, Eugène Delacroix, 1824

Salon Sensations

At the 1824 Salon, Delacroix caused a stir with his prize-winning *Massacre at Chios* (left), which showed the massacre of civilians during the Greek War of Independence (1821–1829). He allegedly retouched the background after having seen a preview of Constable's *Hay Wain*. He also borrowed the pyramid composition of Gericault's *Raft of the Medusa*. Delacroix's painting drew both criticism and praise for its gruesome true story, loose brushwork, and bold use of color.

King of Color

Color fascinated Delacroix. He studied the way complementary (opposite) colors look stronger when they're next to each other and was revolutionary in using color in shadows to contrast with areas of light. He also used a wide variety of shades—for example, adding visible greens and blues to pink flesh. Instead of blending, he often interwove colors in bold strokes and flecks. This helped to give his paintings amazing movement and life.

Literature and Liberty

Delacroix loved literature and painted many scenes from Romantic poetry. He also explored themes of liberty and tragedy in real life. One of his most famous works—*Liberty Leading the People* (below)—commemorates the July Revolution of 1830, which overthrew Charles X of France. It was a violent three-day uprising led by the people of Paris.

Symbolic Scene

Liberty Leading the People is an allegorical painting, which means it uses symbols to represent things. Liberty is shown as a woman, fiery and brave, thrusting the French flag victoriously into the air. She forms the peak of another pyramid-shaped composition, with fallen heroes strewn below. The boy beside her is Gavroche, a symbol of youthful rebellion who may have inspired the character in Victor Hugo's *Les Misérables* (1862).

Liberty Leading the People, Eugène Delacroix, 1830

Look Closer

Delacroix used his trademark vigorous brushwork to bring this painting to life. Notice how certain colors echo around the canvas. Where else in the painting can you see the red, blue, and white of the French flag? What makes these colors stand out?

"I have undertaken a modern subject, a barricade, and although I may not have fought for my country, at least I shall have painted for her. It has restored my good spirits."

Letter from Delacroix to his brother, 1830

The **Exotic** East

In 1832 soon after the French conquered Algeria, Delacroix traveled to North Africa. He was one of many European painters who shared a fascination with the Middle East, which they saw as exotic and mysterious. This trend in art became known as Orientalism.

Time for Travel

A few artists traveled beyond Europe in the 1700s, but opportunities increased when Napoleon occupied Egypt (1798–1801) and later the French seized Algeria (1830). Westerners who wanted to experience the "exotic" set off for the Middle East. They included Romantic artists, such as Delacroix and Théodore Chassériau, who found the sun-drenched landscapes, colorful costumes, and unfamiliar lifestyles inspiring.

Stereotypes and Swords

Europeans in the 1800s, especially those who didn't travel, tended to view Middle Eastern culture as primitive or even barbaric. This showed itself in art with stereotypes of savage warriors, for example. But Anne-Louis Girodet was more balanced in his painting of a revolt in Cairo, Egypt (below). Wielding their swords, the French soldiers here are as vicious as the Muslims they fight.

The Revolt at Cairo, Anne-Louis Girodet de Roucy-Trioson, 1810

Look Closer

What makes this painting Romantic? Look at the composition, color, and the way Girodet presents his subject. Compare it to other images of real-life struggles in this book.

Women in Algiers

Delacroix painted plenty of North African horsemen, but he had little access to the women in their private worlds. This glimpse of an Algerian harem (at right) was made from hasty sketches drawn at a distance. Delacroix captured all the sumptuous colors and textures of the women's clothing and the ornate room. But while this isn't a fantastical image, some of the detail will have come from his preconceptions of the Oriental world.

Women of Algiers in Their Apartment, Eugène Delacroix, 1834

Battle of Arab Horsemen Around a Standard, Théodore Chassériau, 1854

Battle Whirl

When Chassériau returned to France from Algeria, he also used his sketches to create paintings. In this frantic battle scene (above), a mass of horseback soldiers swirl in a tight tangle with scimitars swishing and terror in the animals' eyes. Behind them the landscape is roughly but subtly painted so as not to distract from the action. You can clearly see the influence of Delacroix in the energetic brushwork and unblended colors.

Apocalyptic Drama

Volcanic eruptions, biblical floods, catastrophic fires, mass extinction . . . these dramatic ideas all blew up in the first half of the 1800s as new theories on the history of Earth emerged. Naturally they inspired the Romantics!

Catastrophic Theories

A French scientist Georges Cuvier spent a lot of time studying fossils in the early 1800s. He noticed that past species on Earth had been wiped out, and he suggested that this happened from time to time in huge, sudden natural disasters. This theory of "catastrophism" ran alongside religious beliefs, for example in the great flood in the Bible. Romantic writers and artists began to think about these catastrophes and what might happen in the future.

The Great Day of His Wrath, John Martin, 1851–3

The Wrath of God

The English artist John Martin was very famous in his day for paintings of apocalyptic disaster. He knew Cuvier, who sometimes visited his studio, and was also deeply religious. Martin's above painting of a landscape exploding in on itself brings together biblical wonders with geological ideas. It shows a scene of the Last Judgement, where God causes a deadly earthquake—a reminder of human powerlessness against nature and the immortal world.

The Last Day of Pompeii, Karl Briullov, 1830–33

Volcanic Disaster

Martin also captured real-life devastation in a painting of Mount Vesuvius erupting in 79 AD. The eruption buried the nearby city of Pompeii, and excavations were underway there during the Romantic era. Other artists, including Dahl, Turner, and the Russian Karl Briullov, painted this or more recent eruptions of Vesuvius (above). Another volcano, Mount Tambora in Indonesia, also inspired the Romantics after it erupted in 1815 and caused years of global climate change and famine.

Color and Floods

In 1840 a book by the German Romantic Johan Wolfgang von Goethe was translated into English. It was called *Theory of Colors*, and Turner owned a copy. Goethe had groundbreaking ideas about the way color can be used to create moods—he suggested that while reds and yellows are positive and life-enhancing, blues and greens conjure up feelings of anxiety and restlessness. Turner used this theory along with his sweeping brushwork to paint this ominous image of the biblical great flood at right.

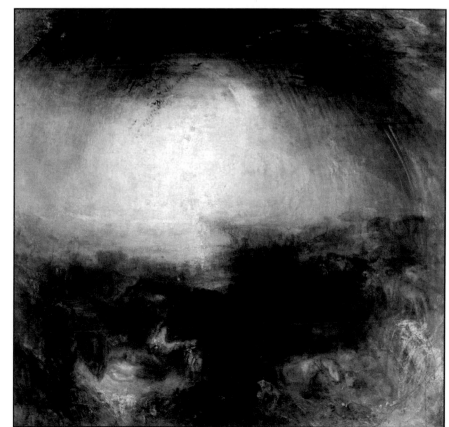

Shade and Darkness – the Evening of the Deluge, J.M.W. Turner, 1843

Romanticism in Stone

With all its energy and emotion, Romanticism was better suited to painting than to the heavy materials of traditional sculpture. But there were some artists who broke the mold and produced Romanticism in bronze or stone.

The Arc de Triomphe

In 1836 King Louis-Philippe of France unveiled the Arc de Triomphe in Paris. This memorial arch, originally commissioned by Napoleon, was decorated with sculptural images. Everyone agreed that one in particular stood out—*La Marseillaise* by François Rude (below). It was bursting with the epic dynamism of paintings like Delacroix's *Liberty Leading the People*.

La Marseillaise (The Departure of the Volunteers of 1792), François Rude, 1833–1836

Rousing Sculpture

Rude's sculpture carries the familiar Romantic theme of French revolutionaries rallying for freedom. The armed citizens, from young to old, are rippling with movement and feeling. At the top, the passionate figure of Liberty is a female warrior like Delacroix's. Rude captured the character of France's rousing national anthem, which became the revolutionary battle cry.

Exhibition Pieces

Public commissions like decorating the Arc were important to sculptors, though usually in the neoclassical style. Like all artists, sculptors relied heavily on the Academy exhibitions. Often they would make an exhibition piece in plaster, then seek orders from collectors for marble or bronze replicas. Auguste Préault showed the plaster version of *Killing* (right) at the Paris Salon in 1834.

Killing, Auguste Préault, 1834

⤷ *Look Closer*

Préault didn't name *Killing* as any particular event, but it conveys extreme anguish. How did the artist achieve this effect? Can you see similarities with other Romantic work, for example Géricault's *The Raft of the Medusa* on page 20?

Tiger Surprising an Antelope, Antoine-Louis Barye, c.1831

Sublime Animals

Another Frenchman Antoine-Louis Barye became popular for his Romantic animal sculptures. This one at left was probably inspired by the arrival of the first Bengal tiger in Paris in 1831. Barye sketched the animal at the zoo, then made an initial wax model. Capturing the tiger's agility, delicacy, and sheer brute force, he later cast the statue in bronze.

A Woman's Place

All of the artists in this book so far had one thing in common—they were male. A woman's place was traditionally in the home, and though the Enlightenment led people to question their expected roles, it didn't do a lot to help female artists.

Out of the Room

Studying art was very difficult for women in the Romantic era. They couldn't afford lessons unless they came from wealthy families, and even then opportunities were few. The British Royal Academy had two female members, while the French set a limit of four. But to protect their modesty, women were excluded from all-important life drawing classes—in this painting of the British Academy (below), the women are shown as portraits on the wall, while the men are all there in the flesh!

The Academicians of the Royal Academy, Johann Zoffany, 1771–1772

Successful Women

A few female artists did gain success. Élisabeth Vigée Lebrun, for example, was acclaimed for her paintings of nobles, including Queen Marie Antoinette of France. But because women had to play it safe to get work, it was hard for them to experiment with Romanticism. The closest they usually got was in subject matter—such as this painting of a lady mourning the loss of a loved one in the French Revolution (above right).

Look Closer

How does this painting of a woman by a woman compare to other female images in this book? Did male artists depict women differently? Look at their clothes, poses, expressions, and what they represent.

Melancholy, Constance Marie Charpentier, 1801

Christ in the Temple, Marie Ellenrieder, 1849

The Female Nazarene

In 1813 Marie Ellenrieder became the first woman to enroll in a German art academy. Later she went on a study trip to Rome and fell under the influence of the Nazarenes. She began making religious paintings in the style of the Italian Renaissance, like this one of a young Jesus in the temple at Jerusalem (left). This painting ended up in the hands of Queen Victoria, whose husband Prince Albert admired Ellenrieder's work.

Wonderful Writers

Women excelled in one area of Romanticism, and that was literature—especially in Britain. Mary Wollstonecraft wrote about equality and rights for women, while her daughter Mary Shelley became famous for her novel *Frankenstein*, whose Romantic hero is a monster struggling with society and nature. There were many great female Romantic poets, including Charlotte Smith and Joanna Baillie. Some female writers, such as the Brontë sisters, used male pen names to mask their true gender.

A Romantic World

The revolutionary spirit that helped to drive Romanticism wasn't just present in western Europe. It erupted first in the United States, and other countries soon joined in as Napoleonic invasions strengthened people's sense of national pride.

American Nationalism

The American Revolution (1775–1783) was a game-changing war that helped to inspire the revolution in France. It ended British rule in eastern America and led to an independent U.S. A strong sense of nationalism flooded the country, and artists felt it too. From the 1820s to the 1870s, Thomas Cole and other Romantic painters set out to celebrate the uniqueness of the American landscape.

Vast Views

The group became known as the Hudson River School, after the area of New York state where they first worked. Although they were influenced by British and German Romantics, the scenery they painted was huger and wilder than Europe's. They focused on sublime, majestic vistas, including dramatic mountain ranges and Niagara Falls (below). Sketching outdoors, they sometimes combined different views to create make-believe or symbolic scenes.

Niagara, Frederick Church, 1857

Course of Empire

Cole explored human relationships with nature in a series of paintings called *The Course of Empire*. They show man's progression from primitive life to civilization, luxury, and then ruin. The first image is an untamed landscape with barefoot hunters firing their bows. Idyllic farming and urban scenes follow, then war and destruction, until finally we see a decaying city (right), empty of people and crumbling into the wilderness.

Desolation (The Course of Empire), Thomas Cole, 1836

View Across Fjord, Hans Gude, 1859

North and East

On the other side of the Atlantic, Romanticism spread east to Russia, taking in Belgium, Italy, and Poland along the way. It also crept north to Scandinavia, where artists took pride in their harsh but beautiful landscape and special light. The Norwegian Hans Gude, for example, painted vivid views of the fjords around his country's coastline (above). Like other Romantics, he sketched fresh from nature and paid attention to storms and skies.

41

The New Hero

By the mid-1800s, after decades of industrialization, western society had radically changed. The gap between rich and poor had widened, and people felt less idealistic. A movement called Realism emerged in art, alongside new strains of Romanticism.

Changing Society

The Industrial Revolution and the mechanization of farming brought many rural people to the cities. They worked in factories for very low wages, while at the same time, rich business owners became richer. This was underlined in 1848, when the Germans Karl Marx and Friedrich Engels wrote their *Communist Manifesto*. They said that society kept the poor at a permanent disadvantage and called for a new classless system.

The Stone Breakers, Gustave Courbet, 1849

Gritty Realism

The Realist movement, led by French artists like Gustave Courbet, grew out of this focus on working-class struggles. It introduced a new type of hero—not the revolutionary warrior but the humble laborer experiencing the drudgery of everyday life. In contrast to Romantic emotions, realism was blunt and unsentimental. For example, we can't see the expressions on the faces of these two men breaking stones for gravel (above).

The Barbizon School

Despite the move toward realism, the Romantic spirit lived on. In France a group of artists called the Barbizon School took to painting in the countryside around Paris. They inherited the Romantics' passion for nature and an interest in the landscape's mood. But rather than concentrating on awe and wonder, they bridged the gap with realism by painting modest, ordinary scenes like Corot's (right).

The Gust of Wind, Jean-Baptiste-Camille Corot, 1865–1870

A New Brotherhood

In England a more escapist style appeared with the Pre-Raphaelite Brotherhood. These artists studied nature closely too and were also heavily influenced by the Nazarenes. They took inspiration from the Bible and the Middle Ages, as well as themes from literature. This painting shows a scene from *Hamlet* by William Shakespeare—a writer the Romantics idolized.

Ophelia, John Everett Millais, 1851–1852

Look Closer

Millais's model posed for this picture in a bath full of water! The artist spent a long time painting the foliage and flowers around her. Notice all the tiny detail—how does it compare to Nazarene work?

The Romantic Legacy

After the 1850s, Romanticism lost its force as a movement, but that didn't mean it was forgotten! All the restless energy, individual expression, emotion, and deeper meaning of the style had a lasting effect on art.

Myths and Dreams

Toward the end of the 1800s, a group of artists called the Symbolists revived the mystical side of Romanticism. They celebrated spirituality, dreams, and the imagination, trying to paint a deeper reality in scenes like Redon's mythical chariot (right). In the 1920s and 1930s, the surrealists also explored dreams and the subconscious, rejecting rational thinking just as the Romantics did. Both movements brought a new, modern feel to Romantic ideas.

Chariot of Apollo, Odilon Redon, c.1908

Western Hills, Graham Sutherland, 1938–1941

Emotional Landscapes

Around the time of World War II (1939–1945), some British artists looked emotionally again at the landscape. Paul Nash, Graham Sutherland, and others became known as Neo-Romantics. Sutherland sketched outdoors but moved away from what his eyes had seen when he finished paintings in his studio. *Western Hills* (left) is more an atmospheric memory than a direct observation—Sutherland called it "paraphrasing nature."

Individual Impact

The Romantic artists had an equally important influence as individuals. Constable and Turner's sketches were often abstract in all but name and had a huge impact on modern painting. The immediacy of their art, as well as Delacroix's color and brushwork, inspired impressionists like Monet (below) to develop their famous dappled style. Many future artists looked to Goya for intense emotion or Friedrich for spiritual splendor.

Stormy Sea in Étretat, Claude Monet, 1883

The Artist's Voice

The idea of the artist as a free spirit, rebel, and visionary also began with Romanticism. Painters and sculptors became a voice of their time, commenting on politics, beliefs, and events. They offered a personal response to the world, including nostalgia for nature as industry and technology advanced. All of these ideals are still very important in art, life, and culture today!

Glossary

abstract—not representing an actual object, place, or living thing

altarpiece—an artwork designed to be set above and behind a church altar

apocalyptic—relating to the end of the world

blasphemy—showing offense to God or sacred things

canvas—a strong type of fabric that many artists use to paint on

classical—relating to ancient Greek and Roman culture

commission—a work that is made to order

composition—the way parts of a picture or sculpture are arranged

court painter—an artist who worked for a royal or noble family

Enlightenment—a European intellectual movement (c.1650-1800) that promoted reason, logic, and individual thinking

etching—a print made from a design engraved on a sheet of metal

fresco—a type of wall painting made directly onto wet plaster

idealized—made to look more perfect than reality

Industrial Revolution—the rapid development of industry and mechanization

landscape painting—depicting natural scenery as the main subject

medieval—relating to the Middle Ages, the period from c.1000 to the 1450s

mythical—to do with traditional stories known as myths

naturalistic—closely imitating real life or nature

neoclassicism—a movement in painting and other arts in Europe (c.1760–1850) that drew inspiration from ancient Greece and Rome

paraphrasing—rewording

patron—a person who supports someone financially

perspective—the art of showing three-dimensional objects on a flat surface, creating the effect of depth and distance

pigment—a type of coloring, usually in powdered form, that forms the basis of paint

preconception—an idea or opinion formed before having enough information about it

propaganda—information or imagery, often biased or misleading, that is used to promote a particular person or cause

Protestant Reformation—a 16th century movement that tried to reform the Roman Catholic Church

replica—an exact copy

rococo—a playful, ornamental art style that flourished in Europe in the mid-1700s

scimitar—a curved sword

sketch—a rough drawing or painting done in preparation for a finished work

studio—an artist's workplace

subconscious—the part of our brain that is responsible for feelings and things we do automatically

supernatural—things that are thought to exist beyond scientific understanding

superstition—belief in something that is considered irrational, such as magic or the supernatural

surrealists—members of an art movement (c.1924–1966) that focused on the subconscious mind and the odd images of dreams

symbolists—a group of artists (c.1880–1910) who believed that art should reflect ideas, imagination, and emotions, rather than copying the natural world

texture—the feel of a surface, such as rough brick or smooth glass

visionary—having original ideas, often linked to the supernatural or seeing the future

Read More

Books
Gunderson, Jessica. *Romanticism Odysseys in Art.* Mankato, Minn.: Creative Education, 2015.

Riggs, Kate. *What Is Romanticism? Art World.* Mankato, Minn.: Creative Education, 2016.

Internet Sites
The Met: Romanticism
www.metmuseum.org/toah/hd/roma/hd_roma.htm

Tate: Who Is J.M.W. Turner.?
www.tate.org.uk/kids/explore/who-is/who-jmw-turner

Tate: Who Is William Blake?
www.tate.org.uk/kids/explore/who-is/who-william-blake

Timeline

1648 The French Royal Academy of Art is established in Paris.

c.1650 The Age of Enlightenment begins in Europe.

1760s The *Sturm und Drang* (Storm and Stress) movement emerges in German literature. Writers begin to focus on expressing extremes of emotion. The neoclassical art period starts to replace the rococo style. The Industrial Revolution begins in Britain.

1768 The Royal Academy of Art is founded in London with 34 members, including two women.

1770s Artists including the British Henry Fuseli begin making paintings with bizarre or sensational themes at odds with the strict rules of neoclassicism.

1775 The American Revolution begins.

1786 Francisco Goya becomes court painter to the Spanish royal family.

1789 The French Revolution begins. J.M.W. Turner enrolls at the Royal Academy of Art, London.

1790 William Wordsworth and Samuel Taylor Coleridge publish *Lyrical Ballads, with a Few Other Poems*, marking the beginning of Romanticism in English literature.

1793 Goya falls deaf through illness.

1796 Turner exhibits his first oil painting at the Royal Academy— a moody seascape called *Fishermen at Sea*.

1799 The French Revolution ends when Napoleon Bonaparte overthrows the government.

1803 John Crome and others find the Norwich School of landscape painters in England.

1804 Napoleon declares himself emperor of France.

1808 Napoleon turns on Spain. In May, citizens of Madrid rebel and are shot. The Peninsular War begins. In Germany Caspar David Friedrich paints *The Cross in the Mountains*.

1809 A group of German artists form the Brotherhood of Saint Luke, later to be known as the Nazarenes. They revive medieval art and fresco painting.

1810 The Nazarenes move to Rome, Italy. Goya begins his print series, *Disasters of War*. Around this time John Constable starts sketching outdoors in England using oil paints.

1814 Goya makes two emotive paintings of the May 1808 uprisings.

1815 Napoleon is finally defeated at the Battle of Waterloo. The eruption of Mount Tambora inspires Romantic painters.

1816 The French naval ship *Medusa* runs aground off Africa and casts passengers off on an ill-fated raft.

1818-19 Théodore Géricault paints The *Raft of the Medusa*. Lord Byron writes *Mazeppa*. Mary Shelley's *Frankenstein* is published.

1820s The Purismo movement begins in Italy.

1821 Constable develops "skying." He also paints *The Hay Wain*.

1824 Constable's *Hay Wain* wins a medal at the Paris Salon and inspires Eugène Delacroix, who also wins a prize for his *Massacre at Chios*. Géricault dies in Paris.

1825 Thomas Cole founds the Hudson River School of Romantic landscape painters in the U.S.

1828 Goya dies in France.

1830 The July Revolution in Paris overthrows King Charles X of France. Delacroix commemorates this with his famous *Liberty Leading the People*. France conquers Algeria.

1832 Delacroix paints North African scenery and people as part of a European art trend called Orientalism. Barbizon School artists paint in the French landscape.

1836 The Arc de Triomphe is unveiled in Paris, displaying François Rude's *La Marseillaise*.

1837 Constable dies in London.

1840 Johan Wolfgang Goethe writes *Theory of Colors*. Friedrich dies in Dresden.

1841 Screw-cap metal paint tubes are invented.

1848 Karl Marx and Friedrich Engels write their *Communist Manifesto*. Revolutions break out against monarchies across Europe. The Realism art movement begins in France. In England the Pre-Raphaelite Brotherhood is founded.

1851 Turner dies in London.

1860s–70s Impressionist artists begin to paint outdoors.

1863 Delacroix dies in Paris.

Index